Learning to Read: an activity book for children with dyslexia

100 Orton-Gillingham activities to improve reading and writing skills in children with dyslexia

VOLUME 2

Alice T. Lee

Copyright 2021 - All Rights Reserved

Contents of this book may not be reproduced, duplicated or transmitted without direct written permission from the author. Under no circumstances will any legal responsibility or blame be held against the publisher for any reparation, damages or monetary loss due to information herein, either directly o indirectly.

Legal Notice:

You cannot amend, distribute, sell, use, quote or paraphrase any part of the contents within this book without the consent of the author.

Disclaimer Notice:

Please note that the information contained within this document serves only for educational and entertainment purposes. No warranties of any kind are expressed or implied. Readers acknowledge that the author is not engaging in the rendering of legal, financial, medical or professional advice.

INTRODUCTION

The Orton-Gillingham approach helps teach literacy to children who have difficulty reading, through the connections between letters and sounds.

What is new about the Orton-Gillingham method is its highly structured multisensory approach to teaching students how to read, by breaking down reading and spelling into much simpler tasks related to letters and sounds and progressing from them. This means that educators use sight, sound, touch, and movement to help students see how they relate letters and words in a language. For this reason, this methodology is widely used in students with dyslexia.

How does it work?

The first step is to evaluate each student to find out what reading skills they have, their strengths and their weaknesses. This can be done by any specialist or teacher trained in the Orton-Gillingham methodology.

Students then receive instructions in small groups whose members have skills at a similar level. It is important that students master each skill before moving on to the next level. If a student has doubts, the teacher will go over the instructions once again from the beginning. The objective is that the students put into practice by themselves, the skills they have learned in order to decode the words.

In this book, there are several activities based on the Orton-Gillingham methodology that will help the student progress in the decoding of sounds and words.

NAME - _____   DATE - _____

Color the word

BEST

B - red   E - blue   S - green   T - yellow

Write the word

BEST   BEST   BEST

best   best   best

Word Search

b	e	s	t	y	h	n	m	k	l
o	p	z	x	c	b	e	s	t	g
h	n	b	e	s	t	g	h	n	m
k	l	v	b	n	a	q	n	m	o
v	b	e	s	t	g	n	m	k	c
z	x	c	v	b	e	s	t	y	h
n	b	o	l	p	b	e	s	t	v
b	n	b	e	s	t	g	h	y	m

Find the word

best   yellow   under

that   can

best   post   best

best   best

right   about   best

Write a sentence

_____
_____
_____

1

NAME - _____   DATE - _____

Color the word

TO

T - red   O - green

Write the word

TO   TO   TO   TO

to   to   to   to

Word Search

t	o	b	n	m	j	k	l	e	r
g	h	y	t	j	n	t	o	c	z
x	e	q	a	s	h	j	k	l	p
b	n	m	t	o	i	k	l	p	d
f	v	b	t	o	v	c	z	x	h
t	o	f	b	h	n	m	k	l	q
s	c	t	o	n	h	j	k	l	p
v	b	v	f	r	t	o	m	n	k

Find the word

it   to   in

could   think

high   to   this

to   on

just   red   for

Write a sentence

_____

_____

2

NAME - _____ DATE - _____

Color the word

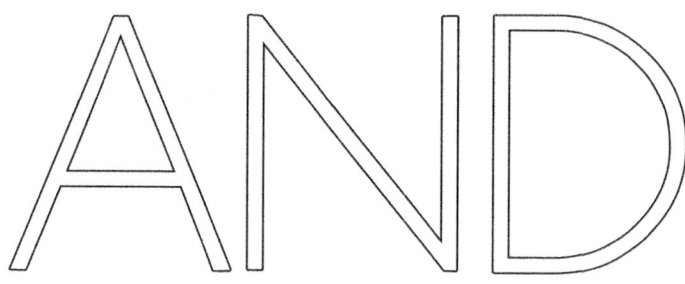

A - orange   N - purple   D - green

Write the word

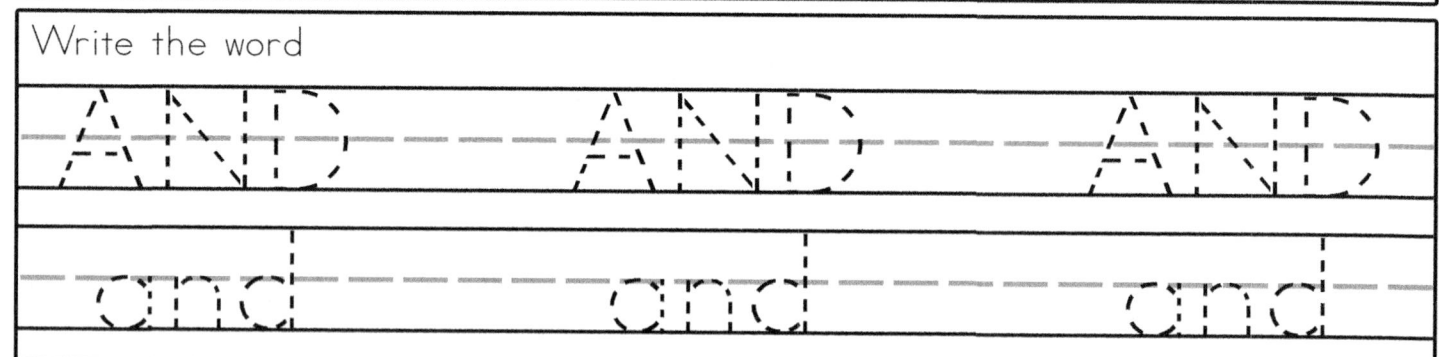

Word Search

a	n	d	v	b	z	x	c	r	t
g	b	n	h	j	m	k	l	o	p
q	c	d	f	v	a	n	d	v	b
n	m	a	n	d	z	x	r	t	m
u	i	b	t	g	n	h	j	i	o
a	n	d	n	b	y	t	a	n	d
v	b	n	m	q	w	e	r	t	i
o	a	n	d	f	g	v	b	k	l

Find the word

an   and   enter

    and   yes

had   down   and

    as   and

and   for   some

Write a sentence

NAME - _____   DATE - _____

Color the word

AT

A - blue   T - pink

Write the word

A T   A T   A T   A T

a t   a t   a t   a t

Word Search

a	t	y	h	j	k	i	o	l	m
s	q	z	x	c	a	t	b	n	h
j	m	a	t	i	o	p	l	a	t
f	v	b	n	m	k	j	u	y	t
r	a	t	v	c	x	z	q	w	o
p	l	n	h	j	k	l	a	t	y
v	f	g	h	j	n	m	k	x	c
s	w	e	a	z	q	w	t	a	t

Find the word

at   go   me

    at   huge

look   at   did

    at   do

for   so   at

Write a sentence

_____

_____

4

NAME - _____   DATE - _____

Color the word

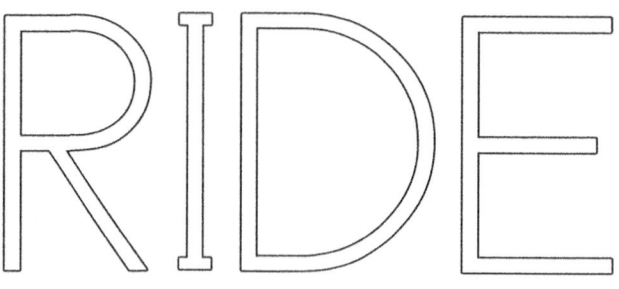

R - green   I - orange   D - black   E - yellow

Write the word

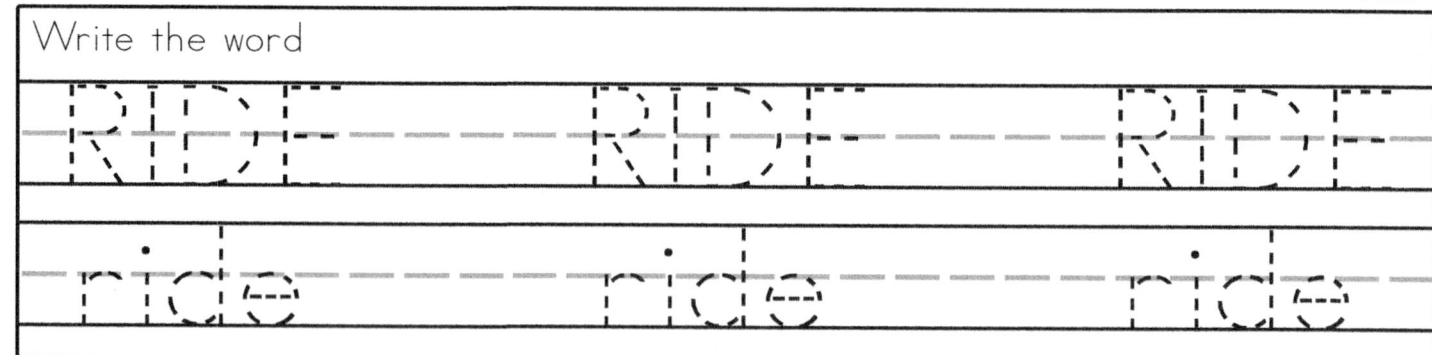

Word Search

o	l	p	r	i	d	e	b	v	n
m	r	i	d	e	q	a	s	z	x
c	v	b	n	m	j	k	l	o	p
t	f	g	b	n	r	i	d	e	r
f	g	j	m	n	r	i	d	e	b
g	v	b	n	r	i	d	e	b	n
m	k	l	c	s	a	q	v	c	b
r	i	d	e	f	g	b	r	o	l

Find the word

ride   some   hide

       can   be

take   a   ride

       ride   which

out   fast   ride

Write a sentence

_____

_____

5

NAME - _____   DATE - _____

Color the word

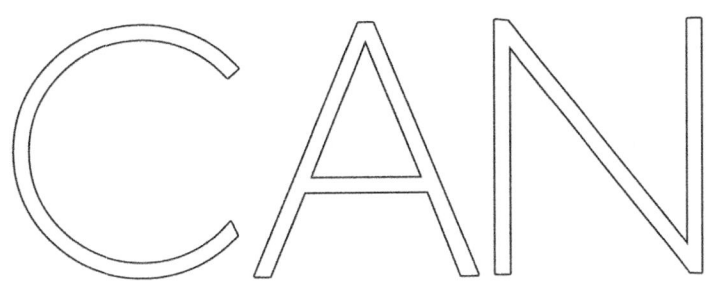

C - black   A - green   N - pink

Write the word

Word Search

c	a	n	b	n	m	j	k	b	t
h	j	m	c	a	n	k	l	o	p
q	a	z	x	c	v	g	b	n	j
m	c	a	n	r	f	g	c	a	n
b	n	t	y	g	h	k	l	q	a
c	a	n	b	t	u	i	o	p	z
x	g	k	l	c	a	n	b	m	r
f	g	c	a	n	y	j	k	l	o

Find the word

pack   can   can

yes   host

can   as   here

can   can

try   blue   can

Write a sentence

NAME - _____   DATE - _____

Color the word

HIM

H - blue   I - orange   M - yellow

Write the word

HIM   HIM   HIM

him   him   him

Word Search

h	i	m	k	l	o	p	h	i	m
k	q	a	v	z	n	h	i	m	v
b	e	f	g	n	j	o	p	z	x
h	i	m	k	l	o	p	s	d	f
g	b	n	h	y	i	m	j	k	n
y	h	i	m	v	d	e	w	s	v
v	b	n	m	h	i	m	v	f	b
g	h	i	m	w	e	z	x	s	a

Find the word

that   him   just

    want   hold

him   them   great

    him   him

go   fear   him

Write a sentence

_____

_____

8

NAME - _____ DATE - _____

Color the word

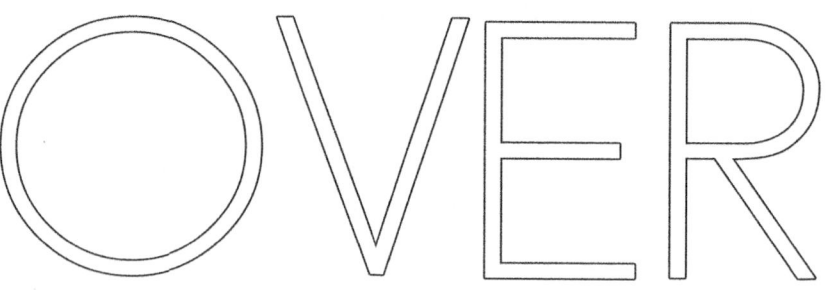

O - blue   V - green   E - yellow   R - pink

Write the word

OVER   OVER   OVER

over   over   over

Word Search

p	l	k	o	v	e	r	n	h	j
m	o	v	e	r	h	n	k	m	l
p	o	x	z	z	a	o	v	e	r
t	h	n	k	l	p	b	n	m	q
a	o	v	e	r	g	h	n	k	m
o	v	e	r	j	n	m	p	q	a
z	v	f	g	j	m	o	v	e	r
b	g	o	v	e	r	h	k	l	c

Find the word

them   over   has

        would   over

far   over   over

        over   gave

open   over   in

Write a sentence

_____

_____

9

NAME - _____   DATE - _____

Color the word

HE

H - blue   E - green

Write the word

HE   HE   HE   HE

he   he   he   he

Word Search

h	e	w	s	d	v	b	n	m	k
l	o	p	n	h	e	r	f	g	b
h	n	u	y	i	o	p	h	e	d
s	a	q	z	c	v	n	m	h	e
j	n	m	k	i	o	l	p	z	x
h	e	v	b	j	n	m	y	u	i
t	s	d	a	h	e	b	g	n	k
l	o	c	v	n	h	e	n	j	m

Find the word

he   just   red

wake   he

had   he   bold

he   class

try   it   he

Write a sentence

10

NAME - _____   DATE - _____

Color the word

SEE

S - red   E - blue   E - green

Write the word

SEE   SEE   SEE

see   see   see

Word Search

s	e	e	r	g	b	n	m	j	k
l	o	p	v	f	g	s	e	e	v
b	n	g	h	t	w	e	d	s	a
z	s	e	e	v	b	j	k	i	o
p	l	v	b	n	m	s	e	e	v
b	c	b	h	t	y	u	i	z	x
s	e	e	f	v	o	p	l	c	v
v	b	g	t	s	e	e	v	b	n

Find the word

soon   see   see

that   can

here   pack   him

see   great

from   see   see

Write a sentence

_____

_____

11

NAME - _____   DATE - _____

Color the word

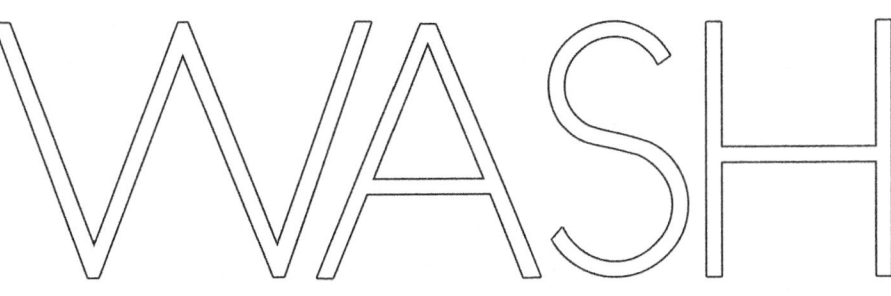

W - blue   A - yellow   S - green   H - orange

Write the word

WASH   WASH   WASH

wash   wash   wash

Word Search

s	d	f	g	h	w	a	s	h	j
k	l	o	p	n	m	j	k	v	f
g	w	a	s	h	y	n	m	k	l
o	p	w	a	s	h	b	n	t	g
f	r	c	x	z	w	a	s	h	n
m	j	k	l	o	p	b	g	t	r
e	w	a	s	h	n	m	j	l	o
w	a	s	h	b	n	j	i	o	p

Find the word

wash   soon   wash

them   that

wash   where   wash

I   am

hold   wash   wash

Write a sentence

_____

_____

12

NAME - _____   DATE - _____

Color the word

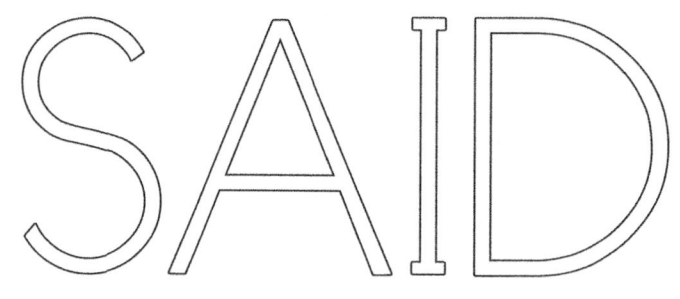

S - red   A - green   I - blue   D - yellow

Write the word

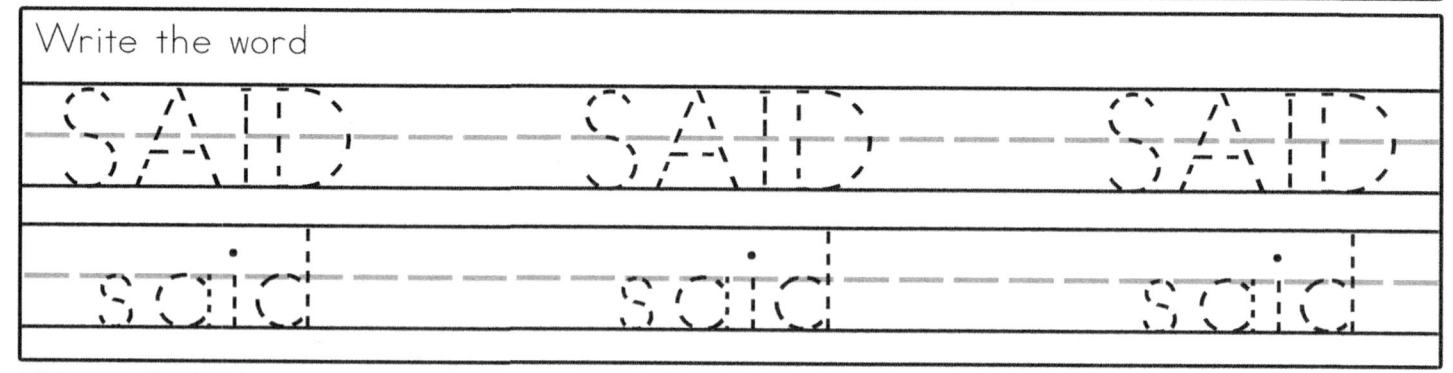

Word Search

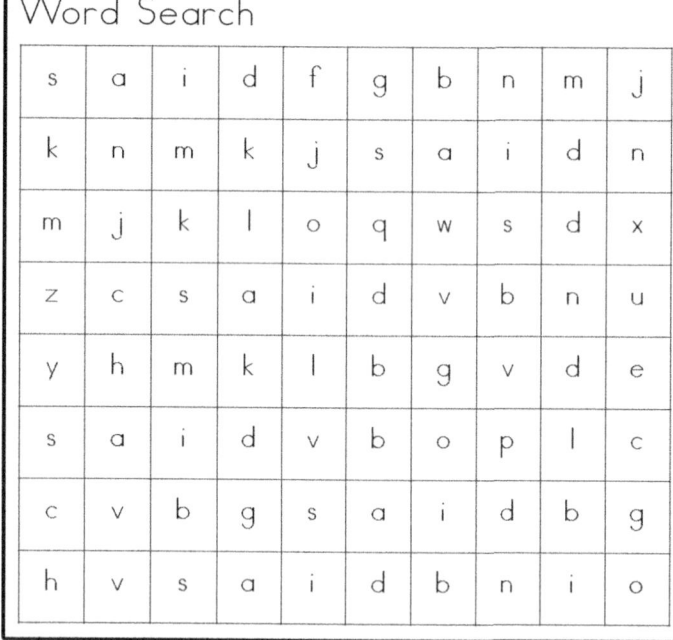

Find the word

said   be   said

       could   think

high   said   this

       it   said

just   red   said

Write a sentence

_____

_____

13

NAME - _____   DATE - _____

Color the word

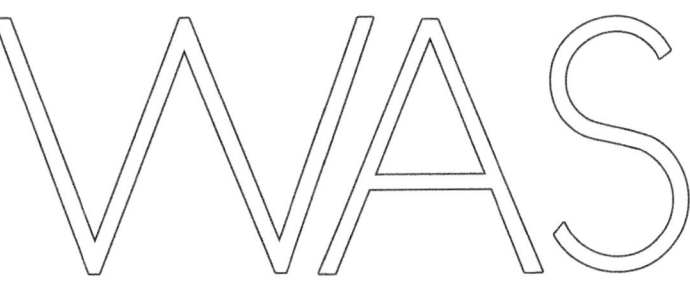

W - blue   A - green   S - yellow

Write the word

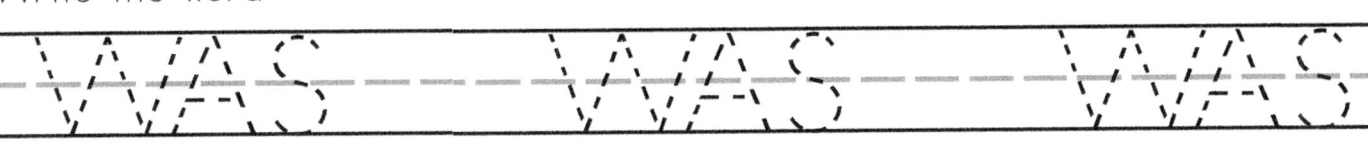

Word Search

s	d	f	w	a	s	b	g	h	n
m	k	j	l	i	o	w	a	s	c
d	x	v	z	a	w	s	d	e	r
g	w	a	s	d	q	w	e	y	u
i	o	p	l	w	a	s	d	v	b
n	m	j	k	n	h	m	w	a	s
x	z	a	s	w	a	s	n	h	j
m	k	i	w	a	s	d	f	c	v

Find the word

was   best   is

would   over

far   was   an

was   done

were   was   was

Write a sentence

_____

_____

14

NAME - _____   DATE - _____

Color the word

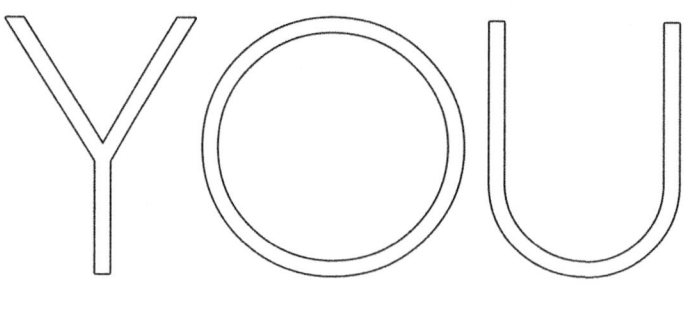

Y - red   O - blue   U - green

Write the word

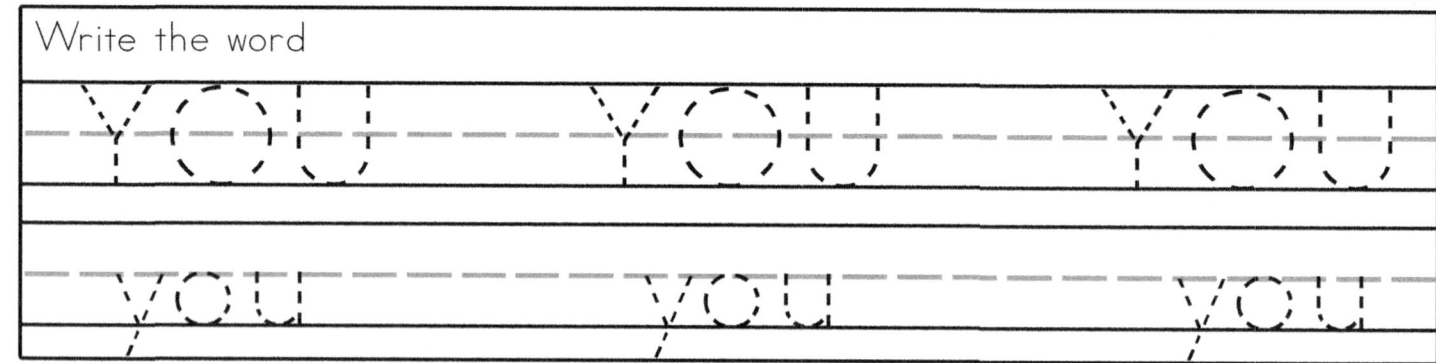

Word Search

i	o	l	y	o	u	w	s	d	f
g	b	y	o	u	v	b	n	m	k
j	d	s	a	z	q	w	e	r	u
y	o	u	i	p	l	k	j	h	d
f	g	b	n	m	y	o	u	q	w
f	g	v	y	o	u	h	n	m	j
k	l	b	g	n	j	u	z	a	w
y	o	u	t	g	b	n	y	o	u

Find the word

you   tear   happy

   want   you

of   from   did

   you   you

her   there   you

Write a sentence

_____

_____

15

NAME - _____ DATE - _____

Color the word

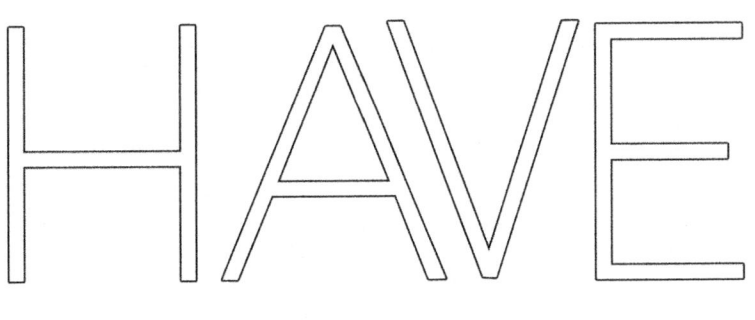

H - red   A - blue   V - green   E - purple

Write the word

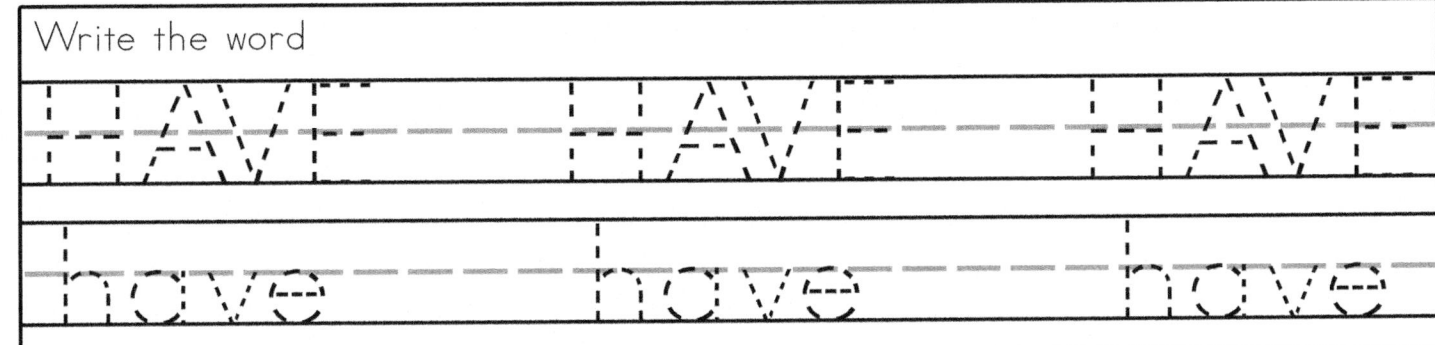

Word Search

h	a	v	e	g	b	n	m	k	l
j	u	i	o	h	a	v	e	d	f
z	x	c	s	d	g	h	a	v	e
j	n	m	h	e	w	q	a	s	f
v	c	h	a	v	e	n	m	i	o
p	b	n	m	x	z	e	q	w	r
h	a	v	e	g	n	b	k	i	o
l	v	f	r	h	a	v	e	n	m

Find the word

see   have   come

have   go

I   could   high

have   put

have   too   let

Write a sentence

_____

_____

16

NAME - _____   DATE - _____

Color the word

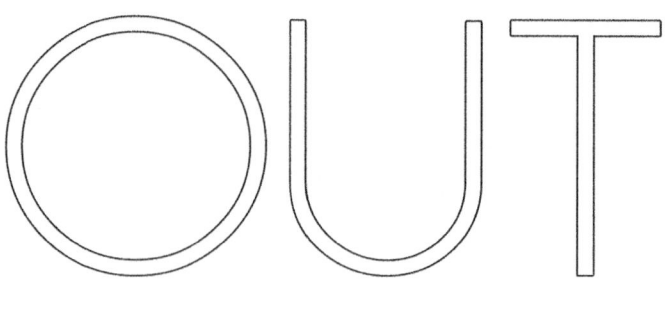

O - black   U - green   T - brown

Write the word

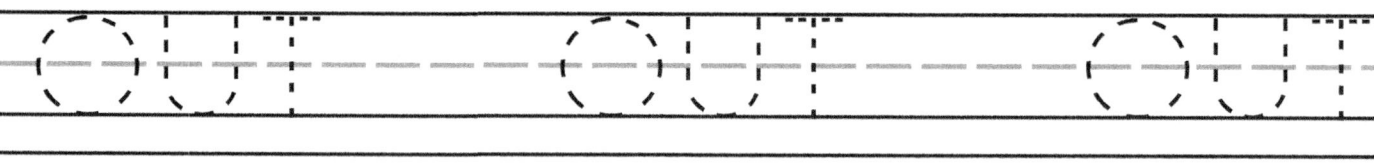

Word Search

t	i	o	l	k	p	o	u	t	r
g	f	b	n	m	o	u	t	v	b
g	f	r	e	d	s	q	a	z	x
o	u	t	h	n	m	j	k	l	o
l	p	o	u	t	r	f	v	b	g
d	c	s	i	o	u	t	b	v	z
x	o	u	t	h	b	n	m	t	g
o	u	t	h	n	b	o	u	t	b

Find the word

start   in   out

      out   so

own   but   out

      those   why

out   on   out

Write a sentence

17

NAME - _____   DATE - _____

Color the word

A - blue   S - yellow   K - purple

Write the word

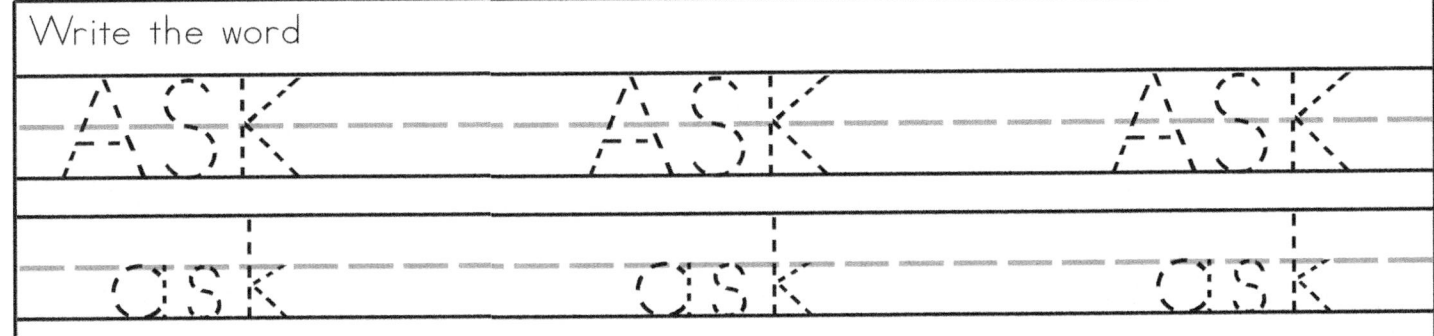

Word Search

g	b	n	a	s	k	l	o	p	i
t	h	a	s	k	f	v	b	a	n
a	s	k	i	o	l	p	n	s	x
z	b	n	m	k	i	a	s	k	n
v	b	n	m	a	s	k	j	u	i
o	p	l	a	s	d	c	v	n	b
a	s	k	l	e	r	q	z	x	b
x	c	f	a	s	k	b	a	s	k

Find the word

ask   done   as

     our   ask

best   ask   ask

     had   ask

ask   can   black

Write a sentence

_____

_____

18

NAME - _____   DATE - _____

Color the word

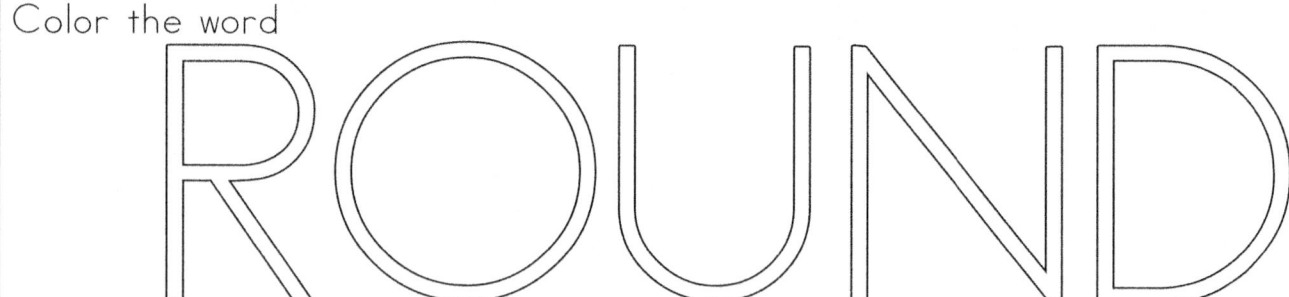

R - red   O - blue   U - green   N - orange   D - purple

Write the word

ROUND   ROUND

round   round   round

Word Search

r	o	u	n	d	v	f	c	b	n
m	k	j	r	o	u	n	d	f	q
w	a	s	d	c	v	b	y	j	g
r	o	u	n	d	m	k	l	o	p
c	d	f	r	o	u	n	d	z	x
s	x	c	v	b	r	o	u	n	d
r	o	u	n	d	f	v	b	m	k
l	c	v	g	r	o	u	n	d	s

Find the word

round   can   best

       yellow   round

has   round   for

       round   sleep

round   once   its

Write a sentence

_____

_____

19

NAME - _____   DATE - _____

Color the word

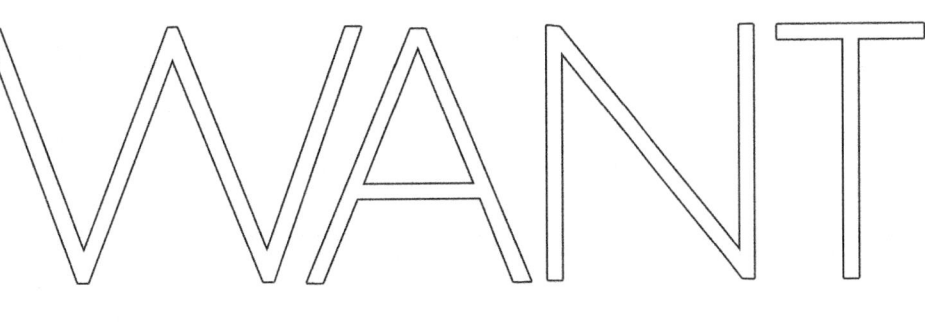

W - blue   A - yellow   N - green   T - orange

Write the word

WANT WANT WANT

want   want   want

Word Search

w	a	n	t	b	n	m	k	l	o
p	t	g	h	w	a	n	t	g	h
b	v	f	d	w	a	n	t	v	c
w	x	a	s	d	f	w	a	n	t
n	h	j	m	k	l	i	o	p	z
w	a	n	t	g	h	b	m	k	i
l	s	x	c	v	w	a	n	t	b
c	v	w	a	n	t	v	f	r	t

Find the word

want   try   your

    soon   want

want   had   our

    that   want

want   where   want

Write a sentence

_____

_____

20

NAME - _____   DATE - _____

Color the heart with the word

some

- some
- take
- some
- best
- think
- are
- my
- some
- some
- some
- for
- some
- own
- here
- some

21

NAME - _____   DATE - _____

Color the heart with the word

upon

as | upon | it

said | his

he | upon | upon

on | into

upon | upon | upon

under | upon

NAME - _____   DATE - _____

Color the heart with the word

very

very   very   very

on   not

where   pink   very

very   could

be   very   from

very   very

23

NAME - _____   DATE - _____

Color the heart with the word
today

- onto
- today
- for
- today
- today
- am
- I
- would
- today
- eat
- all
- did
- today
- today
- there

NAME - _____   DATE - _____

Color the heart with the word
long

long · to · under

long · live

can · long · long

sleep · said

long · long · long

had · their

25

NAME - _____   DATE - _____

Color the heart with the word

make

make	an	make
	most	I
your	make	make
	could	make
said	for	make
	be	make

27

NAME - _____   DATE - _____

Color the heart with the word

pull

here · pull · going

pull · pull

into · pull · pull

pull · as

said · his · make

your · pull

28

NAME - _____   DATE - _____

Color the heart with the word

then

them   these   there

then   into

then   so   then

eat   then

like   little   then

then   then

29

NAME - _____   DATE - _____

Color the heart with the word

does

- does
- would
- ride
- blue
- does
- again
- eat
- can
- you
- does
- does
- did
- have
- does
- done

30

NAME - _____   DATE - _____

Color the heart with the word

put

done   put   did

put   blue

put   put   so

just   here

put   put   pull

put   some

31

NAME - _____ DATE - _____

Color the heart with the word

light

- keep
- light
- sleep
- our
- their
- me
- we
- light
- his
- light
- light
- got
- stop
- light
- off

32

NAME - _____ DATE - _____

Color the heart with the word

pick

your · pick · pink

pick · not

where · pick · would

pick · could

can · pick · for

pick · very

33

NAME - _____   DATE - _____

Color the heart with the word

before

before | best | you

match | before

baby | keep | before

come | before

as | before | have

before | before

34

NAME - _____ DATE - _____

Color the heart with the word

down

- head
- the
- down
- down
- action
- little
- down
- down
- block
- while
- here
- down
- did
- could
- down

NAME - _____ DATE - _____

Color the heart with the word

am

- am
- run
- gentle
- am
- shine
- break
- am
- want
- am
- music
- am
- am
- fruit
- power
- am

36

NAME - _____   DATE - _____

Color the heart with the word

both

both | be | both

power | both

fruit | match | run

both | both

huge | buy | you

both | be

37

NAME - _____ DATE - _____

Color the heart with the word

she

- she
- she
- he
- his
- she
- while
- their
- she
- for
- if
- could
- said
- she
- she
- she

38

NAME - _____   DATE - _____

Color the heart with the word

again

an

again

out

our

again

this

again

it

into

very

again

again

got

again

green

39

NAME - _____   DATE - _____

Color the heart with the word

found

and | did | found

found | from

found | best | found

in | while

found | gone | found

found | there

40

NAME - _____   DATE - _____

Trace the sight word on the left. Draw a line to connect the same word.

very

down

yes

for

it

of

buy

old

yes

it

of

very

old

buy

down

for

41

NAME - _____   DATE - _____

Trace the sight word on the left. Draw a line to connect the same word.

find

only

us

three

brown

now

as

draw

draw

brown

three

only

now

us

find

as

NAME - _____   DATE - _____

Trace the sight word on the left. Draw a line to connect the same word.

call

saw

try

new

had

there

go

am

go

try

there

had

am

new

saw

call

NAME - _____ DATE - _____

Trace the sight word on the left. Draw a line to connect the same word.

funny

better

cut

fall

sit

laugh

live

shall

better

fall

funny

sit

shall

laugh

cut

live

NAME - _____   DATE - _____

Trace the sight word on the left. Draw a line to connect the same word.

apple   baby

baby   bird

back   ball

bear   bell

ball   apple

bed   bear

bell   bed

bird   back

NAME - _____   DATE - _____

Trace the sight word on the left. Draw a line to connect the same word.

birthday

boat

boy

box

bread

brother

cake

car

boat

car

box

cake

brother

bread

boy

birthday

NAME - _____   DATE - _____

Trace the sight word on the left. Draw a line to connect the same word.

cat

chair

chicken

children

christmas

coat

corn

cow

chair

children

coat

cow

cat

corn

christmas

chicken

NAME - _____   DATE - _____

Trace the sight word on the left. Draw a line to connect the same word.

day	doll
dog	duck
doll	eye
dear	dog
duck	egg
egg	farm
eye	dear
farm	day

48

NAME - _____   DATE - _____

Trace the sight word on the left. Draw a line to connect the same word.

farmer

fire

feet

father

fish

floor

flower

game

fish

game

farmer

feet

floor

flower

fire

father

NAME - _____   DATE - _____

Trace the sight word on the left. Draw a line to connect the same word.

garden

girl

good

grass

ground

hand

head

hill

head

garden

grass

girl

good

hill

hand

ground

NAME - _____   DATE - _____

Trace the sight word on the left. Draw a line to connect the same word.

home

horse

house

kitty

leg

letter

man

men

leg

man

home

letter

kitty

horse

men

home

NAME - _____ DATE - _____

Trace the sight word on the left. Draw a line to connect the same word.

milk   night

money   near

morning   milk

mother   nest

name   mother

nest   morning

night   name

near   money

NAME - _____   DATE - _____

Trace the sight word on the left. Draw a line to connect the same word.

paper	rain
party	ring
picture	robin
pig	party
rabbit	picture
rain	paper
ring	pig
robin	rabbit

53

NAME - _____   DATE - _____

Trace the sight word on the left. Draw a line to connect the same word.

school

seed

ship

sheep

shoe

sister

snow

song

song

school

snow

seed

sister

ship

shoe

sheep

NAME - _____ DATE - _____

Trace the sight word on the left. Draw a line to connect the same word.

squirrel

sun

stick

street

table

thing

time

top

time

top

thing

squirrel

sun

table

stick

street

55

NAME - _____ DATE - _____

Trace the sight word on the left. Draw a line to connect the same word.

toy			wind

tree			wood

watch			window

water			toy

way			tree

wind			way

window			water

wood			watch

NAME - _____   DATE - _____

Trace the sight word on the left. Draw a line to connect the same word.

add

food

between

plants

own

below

company

country

company

below

add

between

country

food

own

plants

NAME - _____   DATE - _____

Trace the sight word on the left. Draw a line to connect the same word.

last

never

started

list

city

earth

light

thought

earth

thought

light

last

never

city

started

list

NAME - _____   DATE - _____

Trace the sight word on the left. Draw a line to connect the same word.

story

left

along

might

close

next

hard

open

open

story

hard

left

next

along

close

might

NAME - _____ DATE - _____

Trace the sight word on the left. Draw a line to connect the same word.

group   idea

state   miles

took   walked

sea   group

side   state

miles   side

idea   took

walked   sea

NAME - _____   DATE - _____

Trace the word. Dab or color the word.

face   face   face   face

- idea
- face
- help
- the
- face
- go
- face
- eat
- pick
- face
- face
- had
- face

NAME - _____ DATE - _____

Trace the word. Dab or color the word.

took   took   took   took

- took
- side
- for
- them
- took
- took
- took
- keep
- took
- light
- ask
- took
- took

62

NAME - _____   DATE - _____

Trace the word. Dab or color the word.

once   once   once   once

once   side   once

once   clean

high   might   once

from   once

once   eye   once

63

NAME - _____   DATE - _____

Trace the word. Dab or color the word.

let   let   let   let

- close
- it
- let
- let
- let
- let
- could
- let
- let
- has
- be
- let
- next

64

NAME - _____   DATE - _____

Trace the word. Dab or color the word.

book   book   book   book

book   into   book

out   call

book   bell   book

did   book

book   water   book

NAME - _____   DATE - _____

Trace the word. Dab or color the word.

soon   soon   soon   soon

- be
- soon
- gone
- soon
- few
- saw
- soon
- took
- soon
- night
- fast
- soon
- below

NAME - _____   DATE - _____

Trace the word. Dab or color the word.

until   until   until   until

until	grow	until
under	while	
head	until	until
can	until	
until	did	until

67

NAME - _____   DATE - _____

Trace the word. Dab or color the word.

talk   talk   talk   talk

talk   best   talk

talk   hill

talk   car   talk

talk   open

hard   talk   until

68

NAME - _____   DATE - _____

Trace the word. Dab or color the word.

could   could   could   could

it   could   I

could   an

from   could   help

class   could

could   could   under

NAME - _____   DATE - _____

Trace the word. Dab or color the word.

way   *way*   *way*   *way*

- way
- did
- way
- way
- am
- way
- while
- soon
- way
- hope
- chair
- farm
- light

70

NAME - _____   DATE - _____

Trace the word. Dab or color the word.

then — then — then — then

- if
- then
- may
- high
- then
- then
- then
- said
- go
- floor
- then
- these
- there

71

NAME - _____   DATE - _____

Trace the word. Dab or color the word.

funny   funny   funny   funny

- the
- funny
- music
- funny
- match
- wet
- did
- toe
- funny
- funny
- bat
- funny
- here

72

NAME - _____   DATE - _____

Trace the word. Dab or color the word.

jump   jump   jump   jump

jump   go   jump

high   jump

fear   action   jump

keep   touch

jump   wide   chair

73

NAME - _____ DATE - _____

Trace the word. Dab or color the word.

find --- find --- find --- find

- ring
- find
- find
- where
- hope
- find
- asked
- make
- red
- find
- run
- find
- see

74

NAME - _____ DATE - _____

Trace the word. Dab or color the word.

away   away   away   away

away   keep   away

right   away

any   while   be

away   like

right   away   away

75

NAME - _____   DATE - _____

Trace the word. Dab or color the word.

good   good   good   good

- fill
- good
- best
- good
- does
- and
- good
- good
- my
- we
- good
- our
- good

76

NAME - _____   DATE - _____

Trace the word. Dab or color the word.

from   from   from   from

- from
- did
- own
- into
- from
- it
- can
- from
- from
- from
- far
- from
- break

77

NAME - _____   DATE - _____

Trace the word. Dab or color the word.

have   have   have   have

- ask
- have
- could
- will
- may
- have
- farm
- have
- has
- have
- chair
- open
- hard

78

NAME - _____ DATE - _____

Trace the word. Dab or color the word.

flat flat flat flat

- flat
- done
- flat
- flat
- in
- to
- look
- flat
- here
- big
- flat
- the
- flat

NAME - _____   DATE - _____

Trace the word. Dab or color the word.

when   when   when   when

while   when   where

when   them

for   when   here

when   I

could   when   your

80

NAME - _____   DATE - _____

Unscramble the word and write it on the line.

| both   cold   wish   gave   read   pull |

olcd
_____

erda
_____

tboh
_____

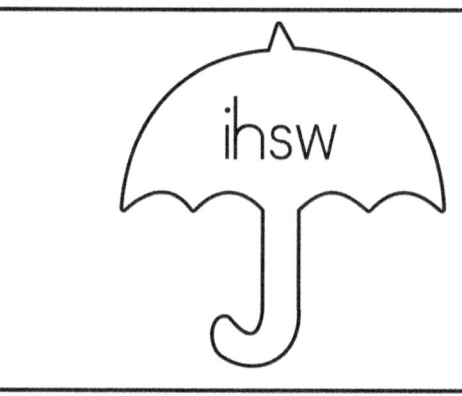
ihsw
_____

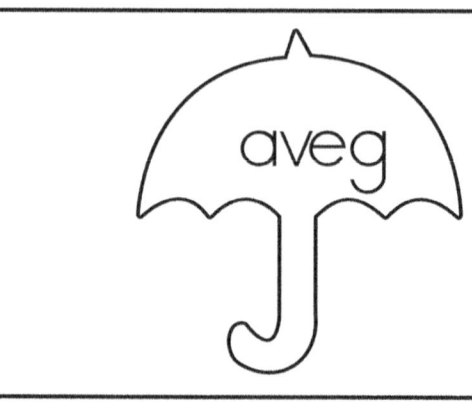
ullp
_____

aveg
_____

NAME - _____ DATE - _____

Unscramble the word and write it on the line.

| made   goes   been   use   very   into |

sue
_____

noti
_____

dmae
_____

nebe
_____

ervy
_____

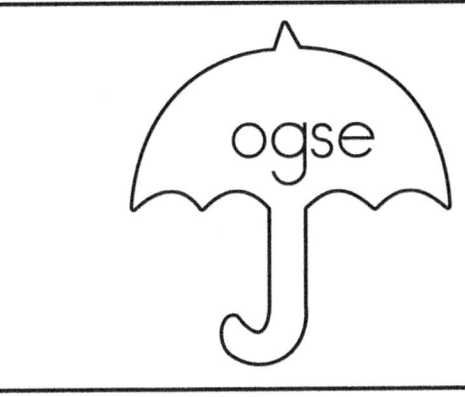
ogse
_____

NAME - _____   DATE - _____

Unscramble the word and write it on the line.

| off   five   sleep   hill   fast   sit |

ivfe

ist

ffo

eelsp

afts

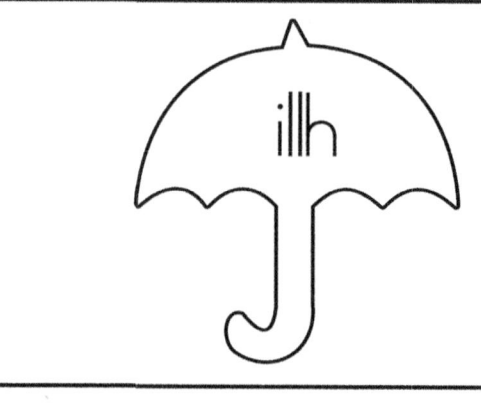
illh

NAME - _____ DATE - _____

Unscramble the word and write it on the line.

| why your tell us sing best |

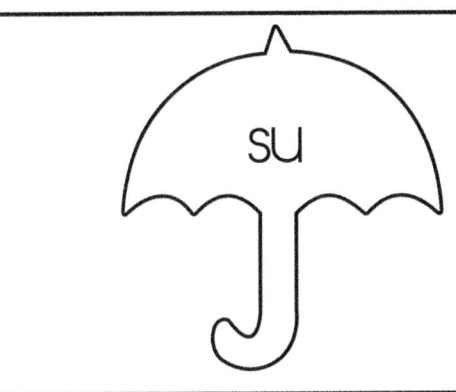

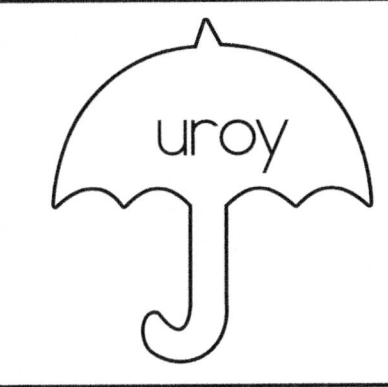

84

NAME - _____   DATE - _____

Unscramble the word and write it on the line.

| the   had   that   one   was   with |

thwi

ahd

_____

noe

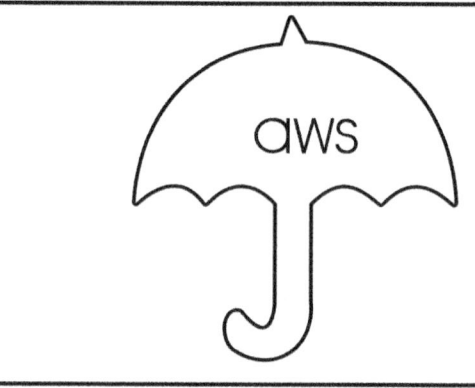
aws

_____

that

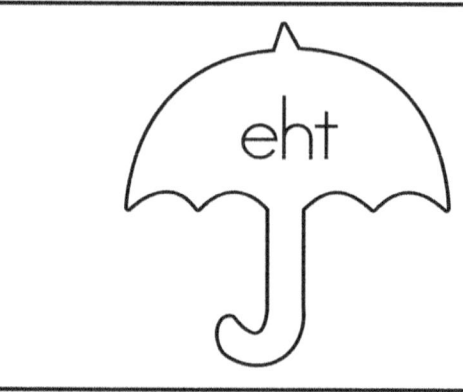
eht

_____

NAME - _____   DATE - _____

Unscramble the word and write it on the line.

| many   time   like   may   her   if |

erh

_____

ikel

_____

aym

_____

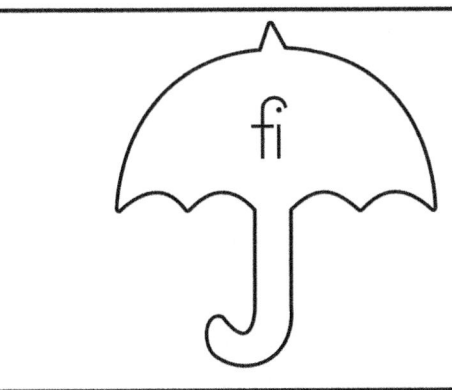
fi

_____

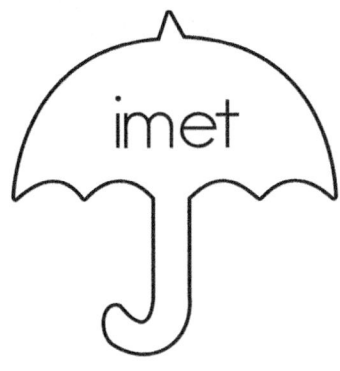
imet

_____

aynm

_____

NAME - _____   DATE - _____

Unscramble the word and write it on the line.

| not but she him our did |

87

NAME - _____   DATE - _____

Unscramble the word and write it on the line.

| part | long | same | two | day | no |

asem
_____

on
_____

ayd
_____

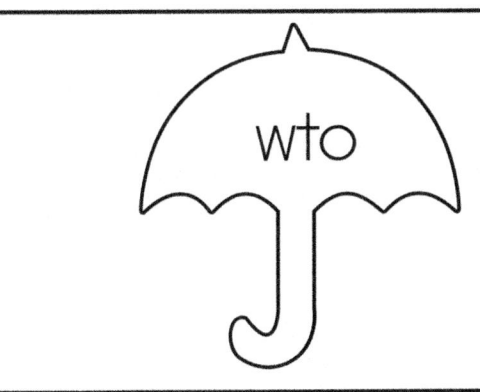
wto
_____

onlg
_____

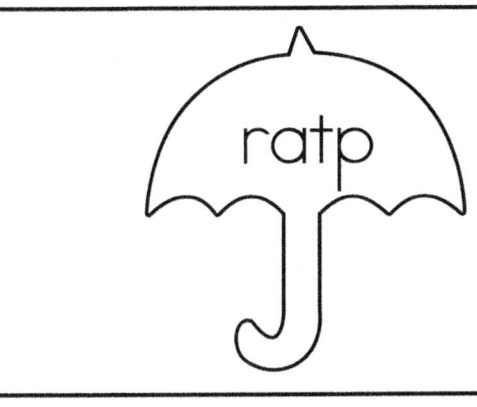
ratp
_____

88

NAME - _____　　　DATE - _____

Unscramble the word and write it on the line.

| back　night　hot　pick　when　for |

oht
_____

orf
_____

akcb
_____

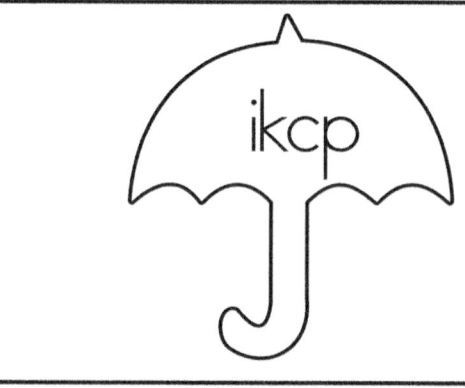
ikcp
_____

ihtng
_____

hwne
_____

NAME - _____ DATE - _____

Unscramble the word and write it on the line.

| each   just   kick   do   man   fun |

_____

_____

_____

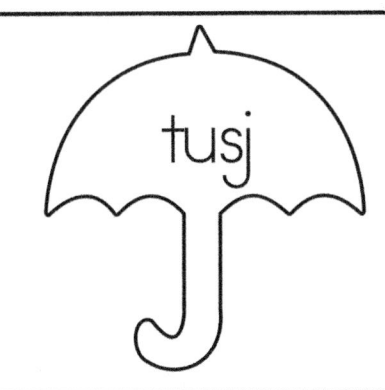
_____

_____

_____

NAME - _____   DATE - _____

Unscramble the word and write it on the line.

| here   too   look   want   while   is |

si

olok

oto

eher

anwt

hliwe

91

NAME - _____ DATE - _____

Unscramble the word and write it on the line.

| yes   pretty   play   from   big   at |

_____ _____

 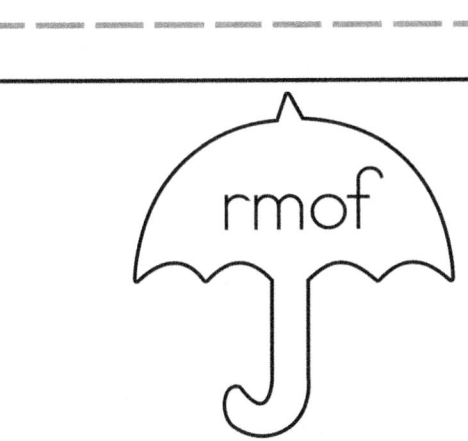

_____ _____

 lapy

_____ _____

NAME - _____   DATE - _____

Unscramble the word and write it on the line.

| ask   has   are   by   cat   brown |

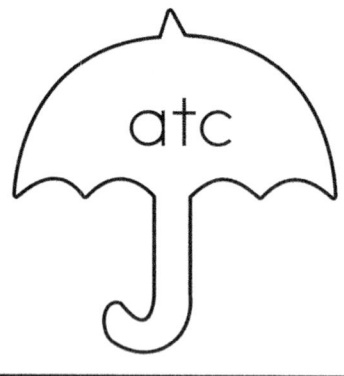

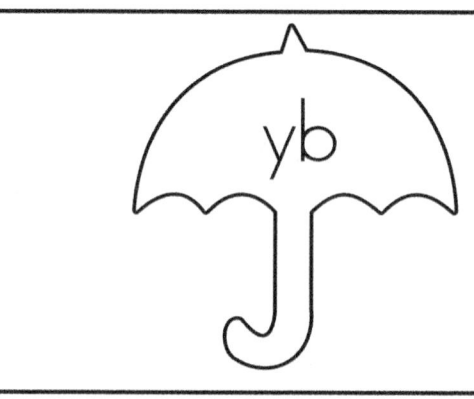

93

NAME - _____   DATE - _____

Unscramble the word and write it on the line.

| good | how | help | me | this | find |

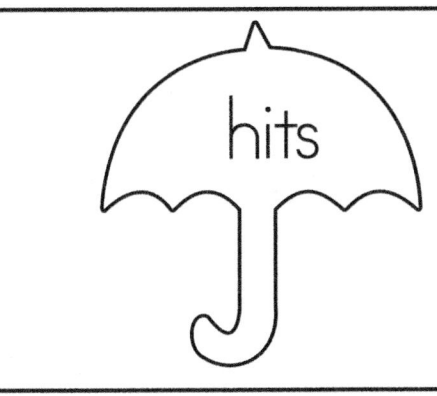

NAME - _____   DATE - _____

Circle the word that names each picture. Then write the word on the line.

fin   (bin)

bin

bee   see

_____

book   look

_____

brick   chick

_____

cherry   carry

_____

head   bread

_____

NAME - _____   DATE - _____

Circle the word that names each picture. Then write the word on the line.

child   mild

bear   tear

horn   corn

fun   bun

fan   man

chair   hair

NAME - _____   DATE - _____

Circle the word that names each picture. Then write the word on the line.

fish   dish

_____

dress   press

_____

donkey   monkey

_____

log   dog

_____

clue   glue

_____

fox   box

_____

NAME - _____   DATE - _____

Circle the word that names each picture. Then write the word on the line.

hug   jug

_____

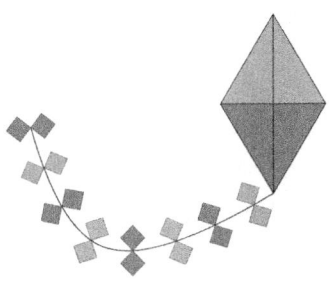

kite   bite

_____

rice   ice

_____

racket   jacket

_____

cat   hat

_____

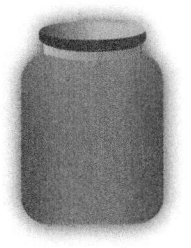

jar   far

_____

NAME - _____   DATE - _____

Circle the word that names each picture. Then write the word on the line.

nut   hut

_____

dog   log

_____

time   lime

_____

pan   can

_____

fig   pig

_____

rest   nest

_____

NAME - _____ DATE - _____

Circle the word that names each picture. Then write the word on the line.

sheep   keep

_____

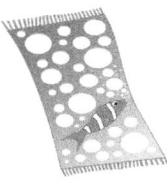

rug   bug

_____

train   rain

_____

habbit   rabbit

_____

tea   sea

_____

mat   rat

_____

Printed in Great Britain
by Amazon